Christmas in America

David Cohen, *Editor & Project Director*
Rick Smolan, *Associate Director*
Mark Rykoff, *Managing Editor*
Jennifer Erwitt, *Associate Editor*
Thomas K. Walker, *Art Director*
J. Curtis Sanburn, *Writer*

*This book was made possible with
the generous assistance of:*

 Eastman Kodak Co.

Lights, camera, Christmas: At the Denver City and County Building

Young dancers with the Pennsylvania Ballet wait backstage during a performance of *The Nutcracker* in Philadelphia.

Seny Norasingh

The Christmas Eve service at Home Moravian Church in Winston-Salem, North Carolina.

First published 1988 by Collins Publishers, Inc.,
San Francisco.

Copyright © 1988 by Collins Publishers, Inc.

ISBN 0-00-215164-2

Library of Congress Cataloging-in-Publication Data.
Main entry under title: Christmas in America.

Cohen, David, 1955-
Christmas in America.

    1. Christmas—United States—Pictorial works.
I. Smolan, Rick.
I. Title.

GT4986.A1C63   1988
394.2' 68282' 0973   88-9583

Printed in Japan   First printing August 1988

10   9   8   7   6   5   4   3   2   1

Christmas in America

Images of the holiday season by 100 of
America's leading photographers

Collins Publishers

J ust when the air turns frosty and the days shrink into darkness, the Christmas season arrives in America. It begins at Thanksgiving—with families, feasts and football. Then, during the next six weeks we shop and decorate, worship and make merry. Our hearts warm in the winter cold. We find compassion for strangers, and we remember there are miracles. Pious or festive or both, we join together in an extraordinary national festival.

Christmas in America is a family album of this festival photographed by one hundred of America's foremost photojournalists. These talented men and women, many veterans of the *Day in the Life of America* project, represent America's leading newspapers and magazines. From Thanksgiving to Epiphany, they scattered across the nation to document how we prepare for, celebrate, survive and clean up after Christmas. Some of them stayed close to home, focusing on their own families and towns. Others went far afield to discover new places and unaccustomed rituals. All together, the photographers took over 150,000 pictures, 150,000 different moments.

The results are as diverse as the American people, as joyous as the season, and as warm and intimate as a family album should be. We hope that you will find some pictures here that capture your holiday memories and feelings, some others that surprise and delight you, and still others that make you pause. Most of all, we hope that you and your family will have a picture perfect Christmas.

Betty Boop tips her hat to Central Park and the start of the Christmas season in the Macy's Thanksgiving Day Parade. Ms. Boop joined the New York parade in 1985.
Photographer:
Kenneth Jarecke
Contact Press Images

Remember me to Herald Square! Snoopy and the Macy's Parade at 34th Street and Broadway, New York City.
Photographer:
Jean-Pierre Laffont, *Sygma*

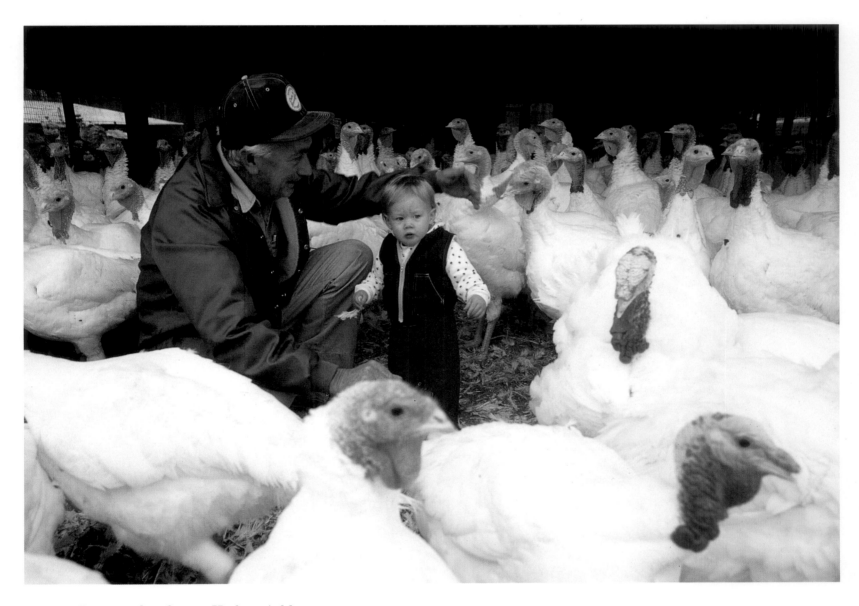

New Jersey turkey farmer Herbert Ashley
introduces grandson Scott to the Christmas
crop of birds.
Photographer:
Paul Solomon, *Wheeler Pictures*

Five-pound fruitcakes-to-be ride a conveyor belt
past the cherry and almond stations on the
assembly line at Grandma's Fruitcake Bakery in
Beatrice, Nebraska. The cakes' fragrant essences
(bourbon, brandy and rum) have already been
stirred into the dough.
Photographer:
Dan White

"His eyes: how they twinkled! his dimples: how merry!
His cheeks were like roses, his nose like a cherry;
His droll little mouth was drawn up like a bow,
And the beard on his chin was as white as the snow."

—from "A Visit from St. Nicholas" by
Clement Clarke Moore, 1823.

Santas from the Dixie Doodle talent agency in Orange, California, strive for just the right look before heading out to the malls. Santas with genuine beards command three times more pay than those who must don fake whiskers.
Photographer:
Elaine Isaacson, *Orange County Register*

This gathering of Santas marks the kick-off of the Sidewalk Santa Campaign in New York City, sponsored by the Volunteers of America.

New York, like most American cities, hosts dozens of Santas during the holiday season. But in 1948, the Boston city council introduced a resolution asking the mayor to designate an official Saint Nick for the entire city. As one councilman said, "there is a Santa on every corner and the children are beginning to wonder." The request was denied, and the problem of multiple Santas lingers.

These Santas are recruited from the VOA's Men's Rehabilitation Center, which offers job training and alcohol rehabilitation to New York's homeless men. During the Christmas season, they blanket the city, ringing their bells and coaxing quarters and dollar bills from passers by to help feed, clothe and shelter the homeless.
Photographer:
Jeff Jacobson, *Archive*

At the Hutterite community in Norfolk, Connecticut, Susan Barth braves the slush and cold to get some fresh-baked cookies from the communal kitchen.
Photographer:
Brad Clift, *Hartford Courant*

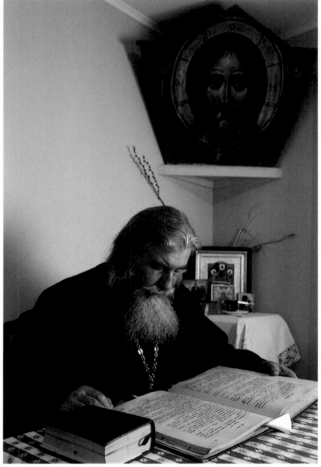

Father Boris Kizenko reads from the Book of Psalms in the rectory of St. Vladimir's Memorial Church in Cassville, New Jersey. According to the Julian calendar used by all Eastern Orthodox churches, Christmas is observed on January 6.
Photographer:
Nina Barnett

It's Saturday, December 12 and time for the annual office Christmas party at John Brady Design Consultants, Pittsburgh, Pennsylvania.
Photographer:
Randy Olson, *Pittsburgh Press*

When the posh Topanga Plaza shopping mall in Canoga Park, California, barred the Salvation Army from soliciting donations on its property, the Army's stubborn corps simply moved out to the parking lot entrance.

Cadet Leslye Hall says she got her idea for the pole net from Matthew 4:19: "And He said to them, 'Follow me and I will make you fishers of men.'"

Photographer:
Olga Shalygin, *Los Angeles Daily News*

Volunteers from the Robert H. Schuller Ministries in Garden Grove, California, stuff 15,000 "Merry Christmas" boxes for inmates at the state prison facilities in Chino. Each carton includes a dozen home-baked cookies, a Christmas card, a poem and a prayer.

Photographer:
Rick Rickman, *Orange County Register*

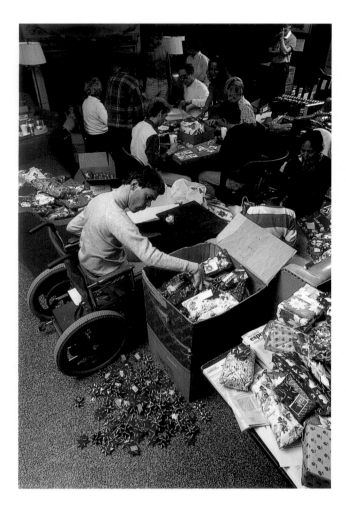

In 1985, a young social worker, Shoshana Arden (behind the table in a red dress), began distributing Christmas presents to needy Philadelphians. By 1987, her gift for gift-giving had become a full-scale community tradition, involving hundreds of donors and volunteers.

Here, Brian J. Woznicki, a 34-year-old computer programmer with cerebral palsy, joins the wrapping party.

"I was with a friend when Shoshana told us about the project," Brian says. "It seemed like a good thing to do, so I came over and offered to do what I could to help. My job is putting the right presents into the right boxes."

Photographer:
Nick Kelsh

orkers prep poinsettia plants for shipment in a football-field-sized greenhouse at Color Spot Nursery in Richmond, California. The mid-winter bloomer is a native of central Mexico, where the Aztecs used its red leaves for dye and its sap as a treatment for fever. Seventeenth-century Franciscan friars from Spain began the Mexican tradition of adorning Nativity pageants with banks of poinsettias, which became known as *flores de noche buena*, or flowers of the holy night.

During the 1820s, the United States ambassador to Mexico was an amateur botanist named Joel Poinsett. Fascinated by the red-leafed shrub and its associations with the Nativity, Poinsett sent a few of the plants back to friends in South Carolina, who named the curiosity in his honor. *Photographer:*
Kim Komenich, *San Francisco Examiner*

Dellwood Foods of Yonkers, New York, produces over 3,000 gallons of egg nog a day from early November to late December for sale in the New York metropolitan area. Jerry Grosso checks a conveyor belt as cartons speed their way to market.
Photographer:
Christopher Morris
Black Star

White Christmas: At the height of the season, Ervey Morales flocks about 25 trees a day at the Wolfe Nursery in Dallas, Texas.
Photographer:
David Leeson, *Dallas Morning News*

Window dressing: Young Philadelphian Michael Trice peers through his grandmother's holiday decorations.
Photographer:
Sarah Leen, *Philadelphia Inquirer*

A sheared Scotch pine disappears under a multi-colored coat of flocking at a downtown Los Angeles tree lot.

Tree flocking is a mix of bleached wood pulp, flame retardant, optical brighteners, adhesive and color dyes. The most popular flock color is white, followed by pink and blue. Multicolored trees are "a rarity," according to San Francisco flocking expert Howard Churchill: "Oh, you know, a tree-lot operator might do a multicolored tree to draw customers," he says, "and maybe some yahoo will actually buy it, but they're really not that common.

"A flocked tree is in essence a brighter tree," Churchill says, "which makes a room look more cheerful. You've also got a safer, more flame-retardant tree, and thus a safer family and a safer home."

Photographer:
Peter Essick
University of Missouri

Palm Springs, California.

A $98,500 sable fur coat by couturier James Galanos goes into a window at Neiman-Marcus department store in Dallas. Next to it, a fox- and mink-trimmed Christmas tree.
Photographer:
David Leeson, *Dallas Morning News*

In the heart of midtown Manhattan: The Channel Gardens, the skating rink and the Christmas tree at Rockefeller Center.

The first tree on the site was a modest decoration put up by construction workers during the building of the center in 1931. This 75-foot Norway spruce, wrapped in 21,000 lights, was brought into the city from Suffern, New York, 20 miles up the Hudson River.
Photographer:
Michael Melford

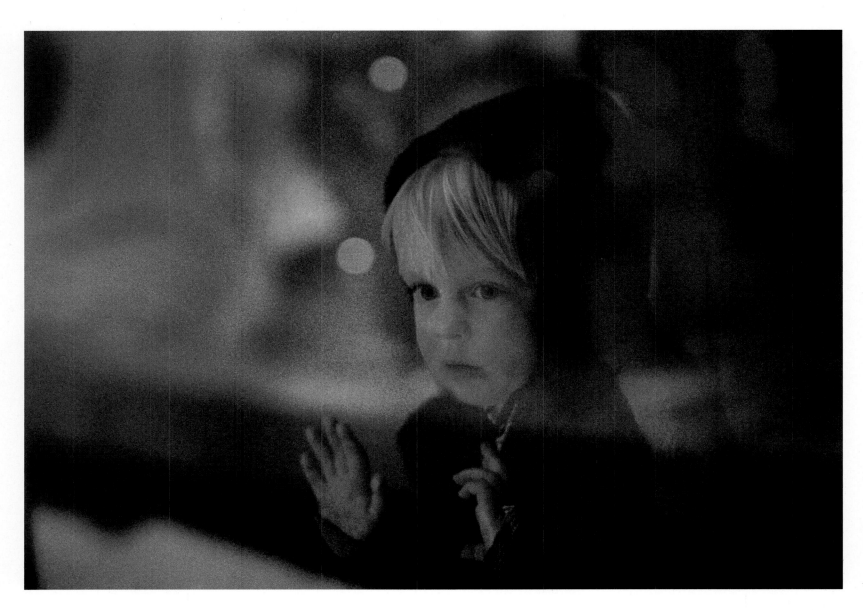

Window shopping: At Christmastime, New York City offers a million and one marvels to tantalize a child's imagination.
Photographer:
Jay Maisel

December in Texas: Ice skaters enjoy the indoor rink at the Galleria shopping mall in suburban Dallas.
Photographer:
Skeeter Hagler, *Dallas Times Herald*

Wrapped packages as big as a child's imagination float through the atrium of the St. Louis Centre in St. Louis, Missouri.
Photographer:
Gary Bohn
St. Louis Post-Dispatch

Fifteen-month-old Amy Neff pulls out from behind a slow-moving shopping cart into heavy traffic in the housewares aisle at Kmart in San Jose, California.
Photographer:
Judy Griesedieck
San Jose Mercury News

Kindergartners on their way home from school in Cannon Beach, Oregon, show off their Santa pictures.
Photographer:
Jimi Lott, *Seattle Times*

On the Saturday before Christmas, things are just about out of control at the Toys "R" Us store in Paramus, New Jersey.

Between November 1 and December 31, moms, dads, uncles, aunts and grandparents spend $1.25 billion at the chain's 313 stores.
Photographer:
Nina Barnett

On a typical December day, over 300,000 parcel-post packages move through the Washington Bulk Mail Center outside Washington, D.C.

Here, Delbert Tullius, a processing equipment technician, unclogs parcels jamming the slide ramp that leads into the high-speed induction sorting system. Parcel volume at the center increases 50 percent during the holiday season, but Tullius says it seems like a lot more.

Photographer:
Bill Ballenberg

I didn't have the Christmas spirit," says mail- man Steve Hudson of Lincoln, Nebraska. "With all the heavy mail and the long hours, you really get tired. So I dressed up as Santa Claus. It gets me through the Christmas season. Everybody loves it. One of my customers started laughing so hard she almost drove into a ditch. Macho guys start acting like little kids.

"Our postmaster doesn't mind; in fact, he enjoys it, mostly because of the public relations. A news-paper reporter asked me if I was having fun. I told him, 'Yeah, but wait until Easter!' "
Photographer:
Kenneth Jarecke
Contact Press Images

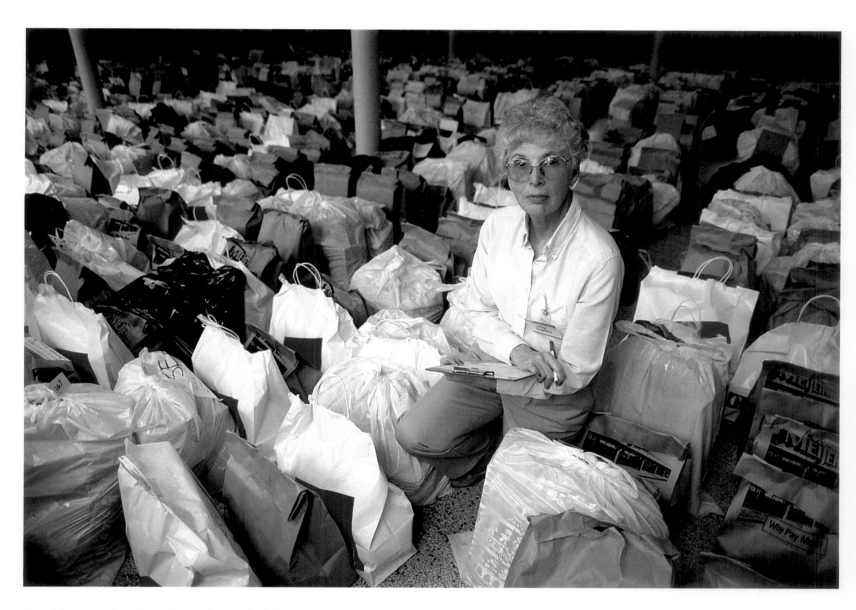

Inside every bag is a piece of new clothing, a new toy or game, knitted mittens and candy; all of it gathered, Christmas-wrapped and packed by the Santa Claus Girls of Grand Rapids, Michigan. Phyllis Scanlon, president of the volunteer group, oversees the project, which puts presents under the tree for 11,500 poor children in Kent County.

Three hundred volunteer drivers deliver the gift bags on the Saturday before Christmas.

Photographer:
Lance E. Wynn, *Grand Rapids Press*

Esprit de Christmas: Soldiers from Fort Detrick unload a truckful of gifts in Emmitsburg, Maryland. The packages will be distributed to needy families.

Photographer:
Bill Wood

Good will to men: Ada Chew serves an early dinner out of the back of her car to the destitute on Skid Row, Fifth and San Pedro, downtown Los Angeles.
Photographer:
Rick Rickman, *Orange County Register*

Capt. Bob Martin of the New Albany, Indiana, Fire Department restores an old tricycle. The trike will eventually find its way to a needy child on Christmas morning.

The fire department's toy restoration and distribution program began 70 years ago; Capt. Martin has been fixing toys for 28 years.
Photographer:
Gary S. Chapman, *Louisville Courier-Journal*

By his own estimation, Bertil E. Valley is one of the busiest Santas in Seattle. The 74-year-old native of Sweden began his 12 years of ho-ho-hoing after a long vacation in England where he didn't feel like shaving. When Valley returned, a neighbor asked him to impersonate St. Nick for his grandchildren, and the rest is history.

Why does he do it? "The love of children. The smiles, the happiness I see in people. Often, even when I'm in my civilian clothes, children look at me and wonder if I'm Santa Claus. Once my wife and I were in Sweden, shopping in a store, and a little girl looked at me funny and asked her mother if I wasn't *Jultomten.*

"Practice? I didn't have to practice, because I love children, I get a big kick out of them. It's just a matter of listening to what they want Santa Claus to bring them, and then being very careful not to promise anything."

Photographer:
Peter Haley, *Tacoma Morning News Tribune*

Los Angeles, Ca.   **Peter Essick**

Orange, Ca.   **Elaine Isaacson**

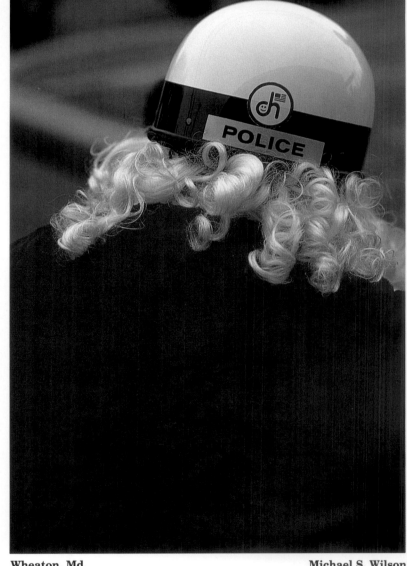

Wheaton, Md.   **Michael S. Wilson**

San Francisco, Ca.   **Steve Ringman**

Richmond, Va.   P. Kevin Morley

Las Vegas, Nev.   G. Steinmetz

Cypress Gardens, Fla.   **George Skene**

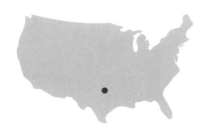

Since their marriage in 1920, John and Gladys Plemmons of Wichita Falls, Texas, have collected over 1,800 Santas of every description including statues, candleholders, mugs, glasses, dolls, ornaments and bookends.

"My aunt gave me my first Santa, way back before I got married," Gladys says. "Since then, I just always loved Santa, that's all I know. I have every Santa you can think of."

Photographer:
Larry C. Price
Philadelphia Inquirer

A few days before Christmas in Pitkin County, Colorado.
The tepee is home to a mountain couple and their children.

The Merced River in Yosemite National Park on the morning before Christmas.

Position Closed

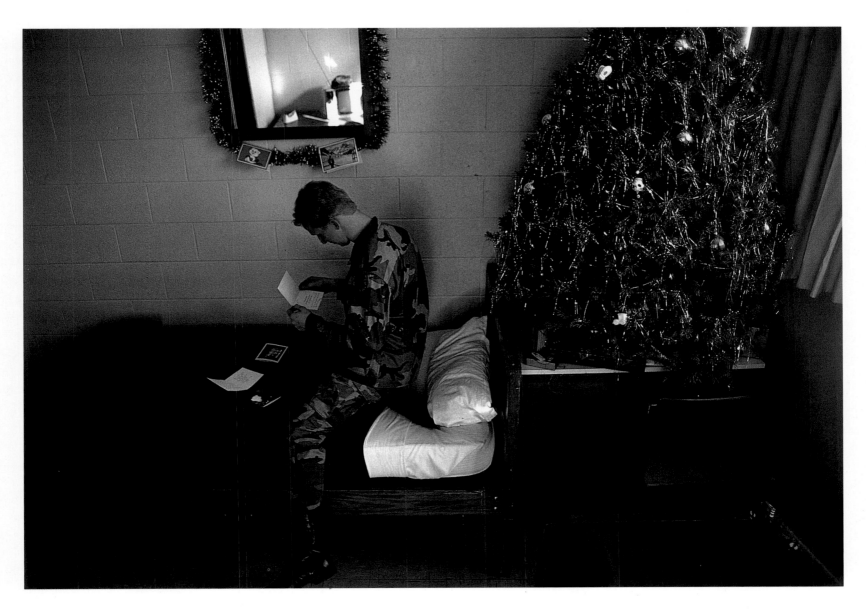

Pvt. Gary Brzovskis of Houston, Texas, spends his first Christmas away from home at Virginia's Fort Eustis Army Base.
Photographer:
Karen Kasmauski, *Wheeler Pictures*

Stacked up at O'Hare: 144,000 last-minute travelers move through Chicago's O'Hare Airport on Christmas Eve, one of the busiest airport's busiest days.
Photographer:
C. Scott Takushi
St. Paul Pioneer Press and Dispatch

Richard Monta, 48, has shuffled in and out of prison most of his life. On Christmas Eve, he was freed from McNeil Island Correctional Center in Washington state, having served 10 years for possession of stolen property as a habitual offender. Released on parole, Monta says he plans to walk the straight and narrow. "I'm not doing life on the installment plan," he says.

Monta (*above*) returns his prison-issued clothing and bedding to a guard station at the prison.

Champagne, tinsel and lots of relatives greet Monta back at his sister's house near Tacoma (*right*). Here, he hugs his nephew, Michael Bolieu and Michael's wife, Ramona, while sister Faye looks on.

Photographer:
Peter Haley, *Tacoma Morning News Tribune*

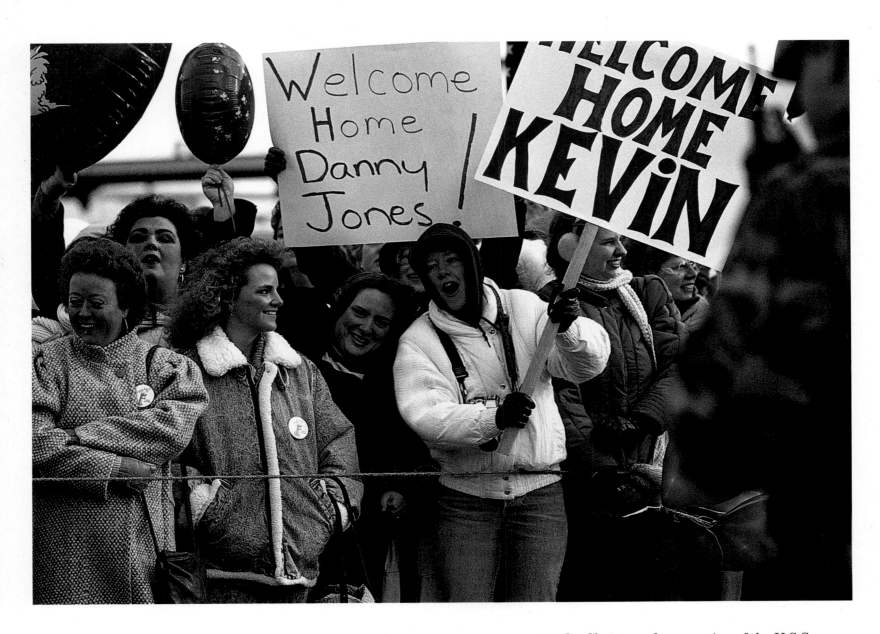

The Christmas homecoming of the U.S.S. Guadalcanal at Norfolk, Virginia, one week before Christmas. The helicopter assault ship and crew of 800 were returning from a six-month deployment with the Sixth Fleet in the Mediterranean Sea and Persian Gulf.
Photographer:
Karen Kasmauski, *Wheeler Pictures*

Andrew Fiederlein, 9, is the youngest of 400 tuba-tooters at the annual Tuba Christmas concert at Rockefeller Center in New York City.
One hundred cities in the United States and Canada now host tuba choirs at Christmas-time, all of them organized by Harvey Phillips, Distinguished Professor of Music at Indiana University. Phillips started the concerts as a tribute to the world's greatest tubaist, William Bell, who was born on Christmas Day, 1902.
Photographer:
Misha Erwitt, *New York Daily News*

A board the Veterans of Foreign
Wars float in Fulton, Missouri's
annual Christmas parade.
Photographer:
Peter Essick
University of Missouri

I wanted to be with my daughter, Victoria, in the parade. That's important, to do things with your children. And I was a majorette in high school myself," says Jackie Billingslea, 27, dressed as a baton-twirling clown for the Aliquippa, Pennsylvania, Christmas parade. Behind her, Victoria and the rest of the Tylerette Pom-Pom girls march up Franklin Avenue.

Photographer:
Melissa Farlow, *Pittsburgh Press*

While the Snowflake Chorus waits attentively, seven-year-old Kyle Anders delivers his lines as the town crier in the Christmas play at St. Mary's school, New Albany, Indiana.
Photographer:
Pamela K. Spaulding
Louisville Courier-Journal

Madison, Wisconsin, had just had its worst snowstorm (14 inches) in years, so they had to close most schools and businesses . . . gee, what a shame!
Photographer:
Zane B. Williams

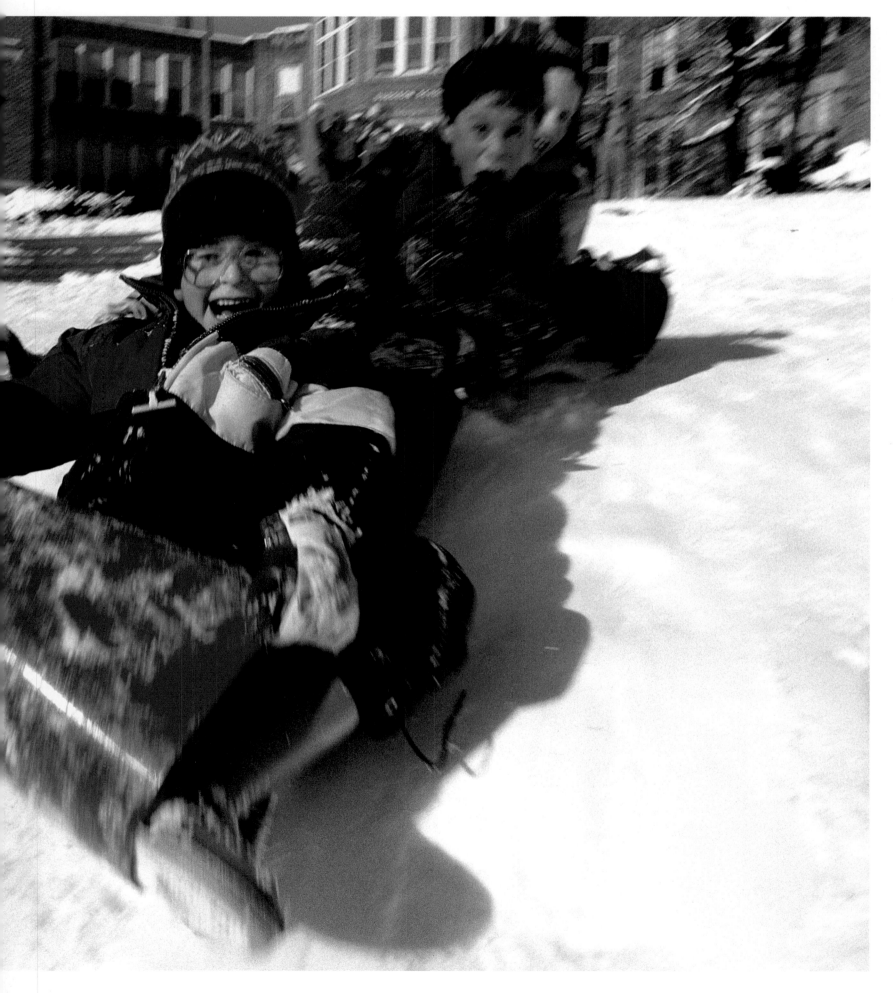

C hoir kids chatter in Fellowship Hall during warm-up for the Christmas candlelight service at the First Presbyterian Church, Haddonfield, New Jersey.

   The baritone on the right, Jamie Barker, 16, has spina bifida, a paralytic condition that is the most common birth defect in the United States. After school, Jamie works as a volunteer at the Bancroft School for children with special needs.

Photographer:
April Saul, *Philadelphia Inquirer*

The Christmas program, "Mr. Grumpy's Toy Shop," underway at Fairmont Elementary School in New Albany, Indiana.
Photographer:
Pamela K. Spaulding
Louisville Courier-Journal

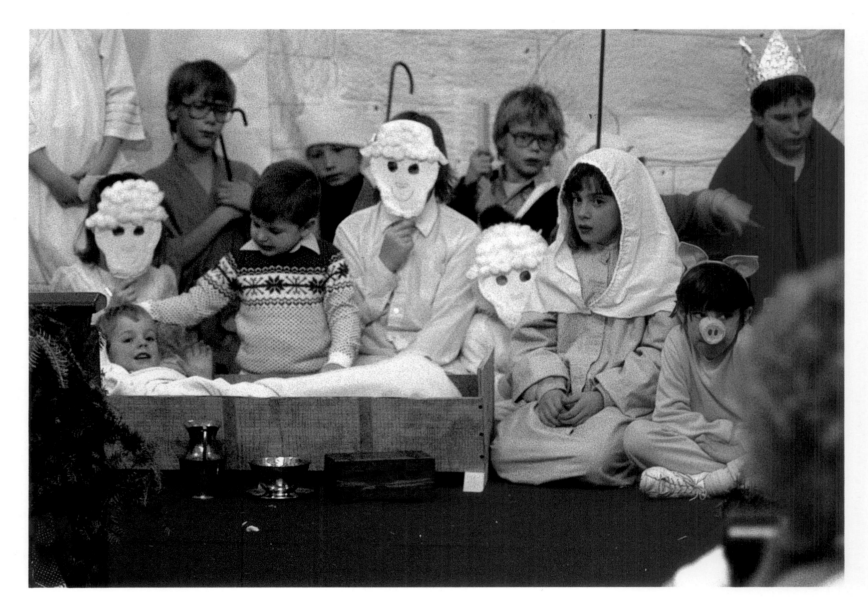

The stable scene from the children's Christmas program at the United Methodist Church, Spragueville, New York.

The farm animals, shepherds and angels had gathered 'round, and the three wise men had just presented the gold, frankincense and myrrh to the Holy Child, when baby Jesus (played by five-year-old Michael Hartle) decided to wave to his real mother in the audience.

Photographer:
Norm Kerr, *Eastman Kodak*

It's beginning to look a lot like Christmas: The first snowfall of the season delights schoolchildren in Syracuse, New York.

Photographer:
Michael Greenlar, *Picture Group*

"What means that star," the Shepherds said,
"That brightens through the rocky glen?"
And angels, answering overhead,
Sang, "Peace on earth, good-will to men!"
            — from "A Christmas Carol"
                by James Russell Lowell, 1888.

Vincent Fisher, 5, and his sister Toni, 7, share the stage at the Father Benedict Justice School in Kansas City, Missouri.
Photographer:
Dan White

Jenny Johnson, 12, is dressed as St. Lucia. According to Swedish custom, she prepares coffee and sweet rolls and, gaily singing the Lucia song, serves breakfast in bed to the rest of the Johnson family in Madison, Wisconsin.

December 13 is known among Swedes as Santa Lucia Day and marks the start of the Swedish Christmas celebration. St. Lucia was a fourth-century Roman beauty martyred when she gave away her considerable dowry to the outlawed Christians. Her unhappy fiancé informed against her, and she was condemned to burn at the stake.
Photographer:
Zane B. Williams

The Christmas Spectacular at New York City's Radio City Music Hall bills itself as "the year's biggest show" casting "the season's warmest glow." As always, the stars of the great stage are the legendary Rockettes, all spit-and-polish precision in the Parade of the Wooden Soldiers.
Photographer:
Dana Fineman, *Sygma*

Young dancers paint themselves into toy soldiers for Act I of the Richmond Ballet's production of *The Nutcracker*.
Photographer:
Joanna B. Pinneo, *Foreign Mission Board*

Roman holiday: Gary Peterson practices imperial posture for his appearance in *The Glory of Christmas*. Perhaps the world's most ambitious reenactment of the Nativity, the show runs for 82 performances at the Crystal Cathedral in Garden Grove, California, and involves a cast of camels, sheep and donkeys as well as 400 humans.
Photographer:
Rick Rickman, *Orange County Register*

Mane street: On New York's Fifth Avenue, one of the famous stone lions which guard the steps of the New York Public Library shows off his holiday finery.
Photographer:
Obremski, *Image Bank*

On Silver Lake near Rochester, Minnesota. Just upstream from the lake, a municipal power plant uses river water to cool its steam turbines. The heated water returns to the river and warms the lake, keeping it free of ice all through Minnesota's deep-freeze winter. As a result, more than 10,000 Canada geese and a troop of ducks shorten their southward migration and spend the winter on Silver Lake's steaming waters.
Photographer:
Joe Rossi
St. Paul Pioneer Press and Dispatch

Dancers wait in the wings for the "Waltz of the Flowers" during the second act of the Richmond Ballet's production of *The Nutcracker*.

Virtually unknown in America until 1954 (when the New York City Ballet introduced a production choreographed by George Balanchine), *The Nutcracker* is now a Christmastime standard for nearly every American ballet company. It is one of the few sure-fire, crowd-pleasing ballets in the dance repertoire, and without it few ballet companies could survive.

Children delight in *The Nutcracker*'s fairy-tale transformations. The ballet is often a child's first serious theater experience, and it has inspired countless youngsters to take ballet lessons with the hope of someday playing a toy soldier, a mouse or even the heroine Clara.

Photographer:
Joanna B. Pinneo
Foreign Mission Board

Cute as she is in her bunny ears, Philadelphian Juliette Coché is actually
in a hurry to change into her angel costume for Act II of the Pennsylvania
Ballet's *Nutcracker*.

Juliette, 9, is dancing three different roles in the ballet. As the only bunny
in the battle scene between the toy soldiers and the mice, she stuffs a cannon
with cheese. When the cannon fires, the cheese distracts the mice, leading to
the victory of the toy soldiers. Then she gets to pull the Mouse King's tail.
Photographer:
Nick Kelsh

A flurry of Snowflakes accumulate backstage during rehearsal for yet another *Nutcracker* in Madison, Wisconsin.
Photographer:
Zane B. Williams

Costumed members of the Northwest Jet-Skiers
Association disrupt the quiet of Puget Sound
near Tacoma, Washington, with a strange update on
the Santa-and-his-reindeer theme.
Photographer:
Peter Haley, *Tacoma Morning News Tribune*

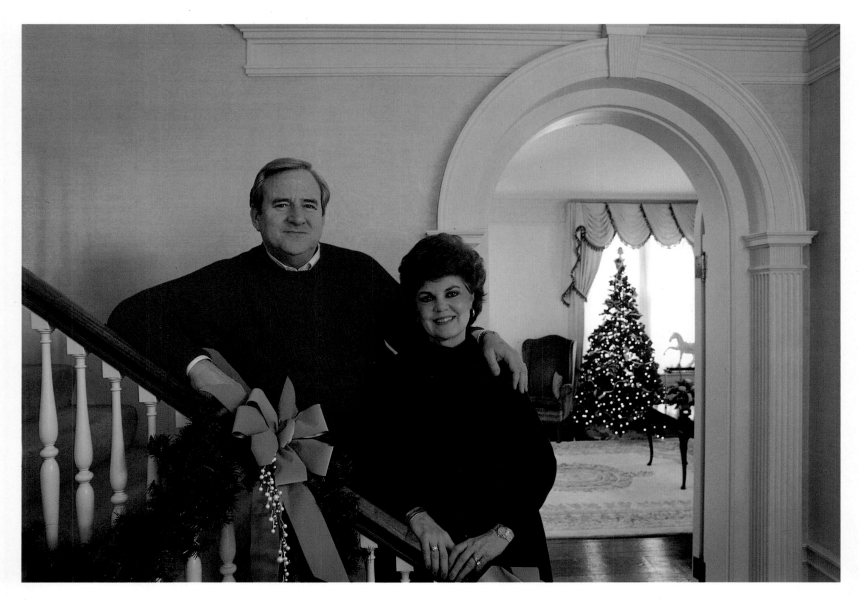

At age 10, Jerry Falwell wanted a Cushman motor scooter for Christmas, but his parents "thought it was the last thing I needed, reckless as I was."

The energetic preacher who once led the right-wing Moral Majority now spends much of his time at home in Lynchburg, Virginia, where he is pastor of Thomas Road Baptist Church and chancellor of Liberty University. His wife, Macel, decorates their antebellum plantation house every season, including the tree, which comes down promptly on New Year's Day.
Photographer:
Bill Ballenberg

Taking a bough: The Twin Singing Christmas Trees at the First Baptist Church in Orlando, Florida. A tradition since 1980, the trees each hold 210 live ornaments.
Photographer:
George Skene, *Orlando Sentinel*

The Spring Creek Lutheran Church north of Marshall, Minnesota, laid its foundation in the northern plains in 1893.
Photographer:
Joe Rossi
St. Paul Pioneer Press and Dispatch

Louise Passman and her two-year-old daughter Casey arrive early for Mass at the Good Shepherd Catholic Church in Beverly Hills, California.
Photographer:
Joy Wolf, *Picture Group*

The reflected glow of the sunset stains a window at St. Rose's Catholic Church in Soldier Creek, South Dakota. Inside, Myrtis Walking Eagle, 14, follows the Christmas Mass.
Photographer:
Don Doll, S.J., *Creighton University*

Photographer Paul Solomon stirs a certain amount of curiosity in the middle of a Christmas hymn at the Milmont Mennonite Church in Milmont, Pennsylvania. Mennonite women sit on one side of the church segregated from the men.

In conformance with instructions in Corinthians, these women never cut their tresses. Scripture also suggests a modesty that keeps their long hair discreetly bundled in fitted veils.

Photographer:
Paul Solomon, *Wheeler Pictures*

This procession begins Midnight Mass at St. Patrick's Cathedral in New York City. White-robed altar servers are followed by several prominent New Yorkers invited to participate as lectors and gift-bearers in the nationally televised service.
Photographer:
Michael Melford

Make a joyful noise: "Mother Mary" Carroway (*center*) leads the singing of "Streets of Gold" during Christmas services at the Lighthouse Church of God and Christ in Los Angeles.
Photographer:
Mark Richards

On December 11, Karen Horger made the five-mile pilgrimage to the top of windy Tortugas Mountain, New Mexico, in honor of Our Lady of Guadalupe. It was Our Lady of Guadalupe's miraculous visitations to an Indian peasant in 1531 that sparked the massive conversion of Spanish America to Catholicism.

Horger holds a traditional *quiotes* made from yucca stalks. Just before sunset, she and 1,500 other pilgrims will climb down the mountain, lighting a series of bonfires or *luminarias* along the way until the entire west face of Tortugas glows in the night sky.
Photographer:
Rick Rickman,
Orange County Register

Alex Joanow, 18, raises the cross skyward after retrieving it from a bayou in Tarpon Springs, Florida.

After reading from the Gospel and sprinkling holy water on the bayou, a bishop of the church hurls the cross into the water. Young men must wait until the cross is in the air before diving after it. According to Greek Orthodox lore, Joanow will be a lucky man for the rest of the year.

The ritual was brought to the United States by Greek immigrants as part of Epiphany Day celebrations held January 6 to commemorate the baptism of Christ.

Photographer:
Seny Norasingh

Ice crystals on a window in St. Marys, Alaska, glisten in the sunlight.

Sunset lights a Russian olive windrow on the Benson farm in Bigelow, southwestern Minnesota.

"On the night of the 23rd," says photographer Joe Rossi, a native Minnesotan, "it started to rain—freezing rain—through Christmas Eve morning. I took a walk through the pastures that night with the Bensons. I was shooting at a slow shutter speed, 1/15th of a second, hand-held. Everything was becoming so dark, but the ice was catching the remaining sunlight as if it was illuminated from within.

"The other reason I shot the picture was that I was at the end of the roll and I wanted to finish it off before I went in. Even if the shot wasn't good enough to be published, I wanted it for myself."
Photographer:
Joe Rossi, *St. Paul Pioneer Press and Dispatch*

Small votive candles, or *farolitos*, outline the Inn at Loretto in Santa Fe, New Mexico.

In the course of the *Christmas in America* project, Kodak, Collins Publishers, WNYC's *Kids America* and the National 4-H Council organized a photo contest for some of America's best young photographers.

When a rare Christmastime snowfall dusted Saguro National Monument near Tuscon, Arizona, sixteen-year-old Alethea Fadala recognized a photo opportunity and snapped this prize-winning shot. For more prizewinners by America's young people, see pages 172, 173.

Photographer:
Alethea Fadala, *National 4-H Council*

A December evening in Aspen, Colorado. Once a mining town, Aspen struck gold again in the late 1950s as a destination for America's most fashionable skiers.
Photographer:
Paul Chesley, *Photographers/Aspen*

One of the busiest corners in New York overloads two nights before Christmas as shoppers flood the Broadway entrance to Macy's, "The World's Largest Store." The great emporium starred in the 1947 classic, *Miracle on 34th Street*, the Hollywood confection that proved once and for all the existence of Santa Claus.
Photographer:
Jerry Valente

Two sidewalk Santas arrive at the 50th Street subway station en route to their posts on Manhattan's Fifth Avenue.
Photographer:
Misha Erwitt
New York Daily News

Christmas arrives in Kingsport, Tennessee, with the heavy chug of diesel engines, a cry of ho-ho! and a shower of gifts from the rear platform of the Santa Claus Express.

Kingsport is the last stop on the Santa Express's 120-mile, eight-hour run through the heart of Appalachia. The train climbs its way through parts of Kentucky, Virginia and Tennessee, through 32 tunnels and some of the nation's poorest areas, including such small, struggling mountain towns as Levisa Junction, Marrowbone, Splashdam and Dungannon. All along the way, Santa and his helpers toss gifts and candy to thousands of people waiting eagerly at trackside.

The Express began its cheerful trip through the hills in 1943 and has become one of the enduring traditions of the American Christmas season. Led by the Kingsport Chamber of Commerce, businesses from the region and from all over the country donate gifts to the Express.

Photographer:

Gary S. Chapman, *Louisville Courier-Journal*

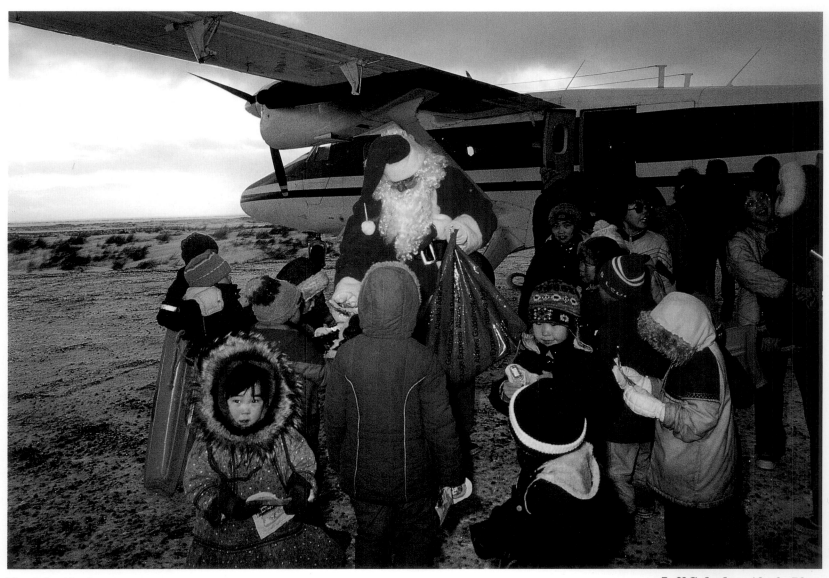

Newtok, Alaska

Jeff Schultz, *AlaskaPhoto*

Wailea, Hawaii

Rick Peterson

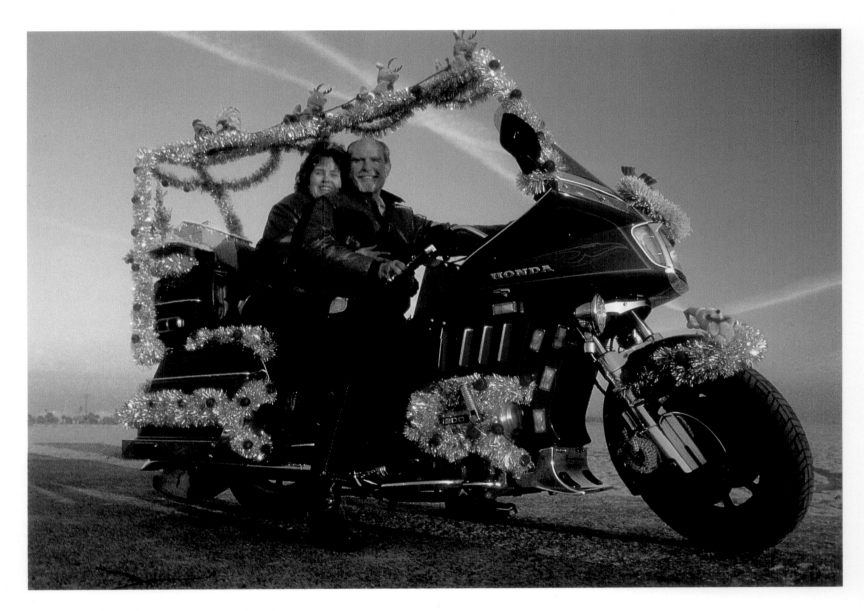

Loyce and William Willis of Garden Grove, California, spent two days decorating this Honda 1200 Gold Wing motorcycle. Overhead, there's a motorized Santa and sleigh that plays Christmas carols. On the back of the bike is a little Christmas cabin tableau. Willis says he does it for the wide-eyed looks kids give him.
Photographer:
Patrick Tehan, *Orange County Register*

Christmas Day above Mount Daly near Snowmass, Colorado: Winds, light and variable; skies clear; temperature, 20°. "It's like a Christmas present to myself," says commercial balloonist Jake Reyna. "Very steerable, the best possible day we could have up here."
Photographer:
Paul Chesley, *Photographers/Aspen*

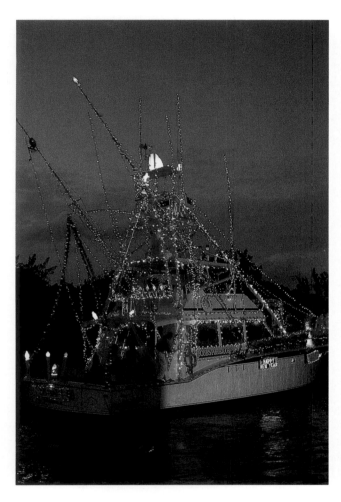

The *Mr. Bobb* motors away from the Miami
Christmas boat parade with all the top
honors. The boat shines with over 14,000 lights
("We lost count," says Mrs. Bobb Messingschlager,
the owner's wife). Once, comedian Bob Hope
asked if he and his wife, Dolores, could come
aboard. A snapshot from their visit to the flashy
yacht was reprinted on the Hopes' Christmas
card, which was sent out to 6,000 of their friends.
Photographer:
J. B. Diederich, *Contact Press Images*

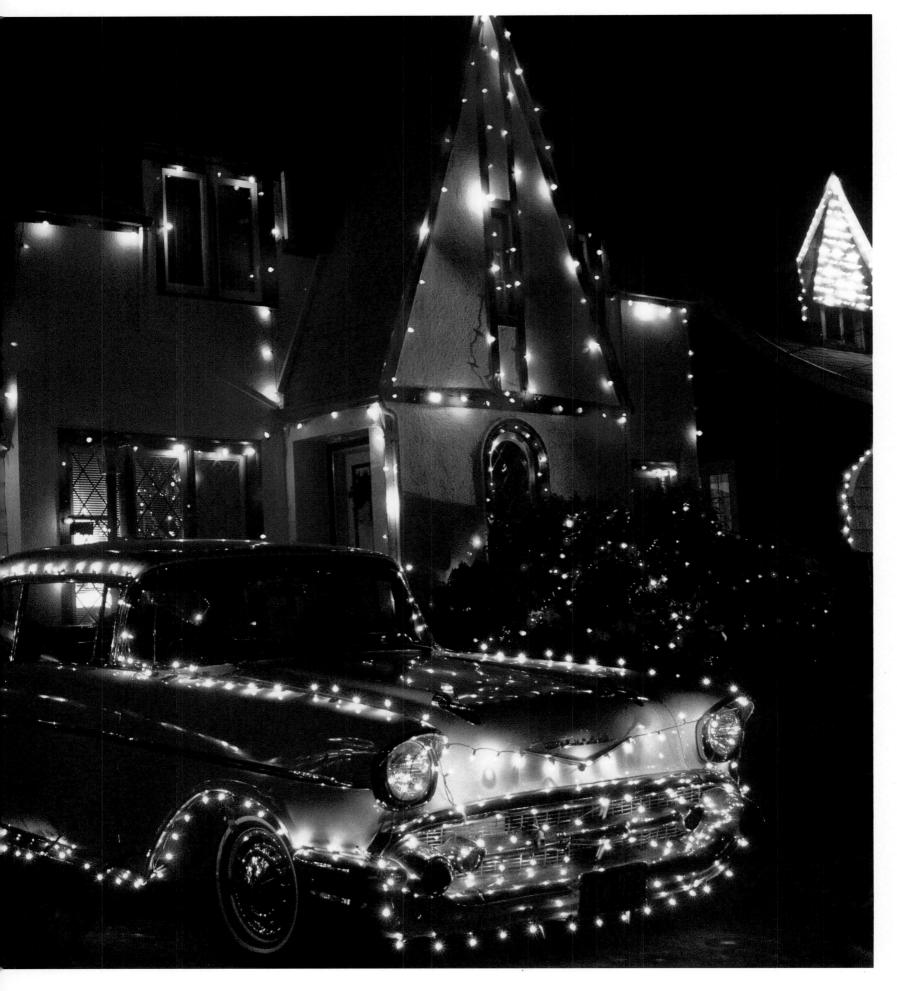

Christmas classic: A '57 Chevrolet Bel-Air struts its stuff on Peacock Lane in Portland, Oregon.
Photographer:
Jeffrey Myers, *FPG International*

Dorothy and Charles Stitham of Marinwood, California, started tinkering with Christmas decorations in 1959. "Each year we try to add something new," says Dorothy, "but space is becoming a problem.

"In 30 years we've created a lasting holiday tradition. The wide-eyed two year olds of the 1960s have returned with their own kids in the 1980s. For us, this seems to be the way Christmas always was and always will be."

Photographer:
Doug Menuez, *Picture Group*

A drizzly Christmas night in New Castle, Delaware, makes the 240,000 lights covering the Faucher property glow a little more luminously.

The National Christmas Tree and the south portico of the White House glitter on a cold Washington evening. A focal point of the nation's Christmas festival, the tree has been lit by the President every year since 1923. The present tree was permanently planted on the Ellipse in 1973.

Christmas trees weren't always in such favor. The 26th president, Theodore Roosevelt, was a serious conservationist who barred the use of cut trees anywhere in the White House. The ban didn't sit well with his sons, Archie and Quentin, who sneaked a tree into their room anyway. Theodore's cousin Franklin, on the other hand, grew Norway spruces for commercial sale at his Hyde Park, New York, estate.

Mamie Eisenhower set a White House record when she filled her home with 26 Christmas trees in 1959.

Photographer:
Kenneth Garrett

Swing-time Christmas at the Madonna Inn, San Luis Obispo, California.

Philadelphia Story: Waltzing into a dreamy blur, young men and women at the Philadelphia Charity Ball celebrate the women's entry into society. A high point of the high-society season, the pre-Christmas affair benefits seven hospitals in the Philadelphia area.
Photographer:
Nick Kelsh

Mattie McCargo of Detroit hosts a party on the last day of *Kwanza*, the seven-day midwinter celebration of African culture and community in America. *Kwanza* (from the Kiswahili word meaning "first" or "first fruits") was started by a Los Angeles teacher of Swahili, Ron Karenga, in the early 1970s. Derived from African harvest festivals, the modern celebration stresses seven principles to guide African-American families: Unity, self-determination, collective work and responsibility, cooperative economics, purpose, creativity, and faith.

The candleholder (*kinara*) in front of McCargo counts the principles—and the days of the festival—with its red, green and black candles.
Photographer:
William DeKay, *Detroit Free Press*

Veteran photographer Jack Corn returned to the family farm in Sumner County, Tennessee, where he found his grandson Austin fascinated by whirring, tinkling star-chimes. Andrew Corn, Austin's father, shares the candlelight.
Photographer:
Jack Corn, *Chicago Tribune*

Dressed for church on Christmas Eve, the Mortons of Warsaw, Virginia, and their granddaughter Katie first open one present each. They save the rest for Christmas morning.
Photographer:
Kenneth Garrett

G rade-schoolers harmonize at a Christmas concert at the Neil Blaisdell Auditorium in Honolulu.
Photographer:
Rick Smolan
Collins Publishers

T wo days before Christmas, Shirley Karnovsky tries to console a call-in at the Samaritans suicide prevention office in Boston.

According to Karnovsky, and contrary to popular belief, there are actually fewer suicides during the holidays, but it's the time of year when family and financial problems can cause otherwise stable people to *feel* suicidal. "The calls are more serious during Christmas," she says.

Photographer:
Stan Grossfeld, *Boston Globe*

146

At the University of Missouri, pianist Michelle Werner leads the caroling at Alpha Gamma Delta during their house decorating party. The idea is to get the girls—and the house itself—in the Christmas spirit before exams start next week. *Photographer:* **Peter Essick**, *University of Missouri*

The Rowley family invited photographer Nick Kelsh to spend Christmas Eve and Christmas morning with them at their home in Philadelphia. Their hospitality made possible this chronicle of a family Christmas, spread over the next few pages. Photographer Kelsh took the holiday portrait below in front of the family tree: (*from left to right*) Jim, Karen, Peter, Monica, Rachel, Alice, Karen, Hannah and Abigail.

At 7:00 p.m. on Christmas Eve, Jim and Karen (*right, above*) gathered the children around the dining room table to light the last Advent candle. At midnight, they placed a figure of Jesus in the middle of the candles.

After the kids went to bed, Dad climbed onto the roof and rapped on the shingles with a broom (*right, below*), hoping to convince the youngest kids that reindeer were shuffling about.

Photo essay by Nick Kelsh

Waiting... At the Rowleys, it's 6:15 a.m. Christmas morning, but Mom and Dad aren't up yet. (They're awake, but they refuse to get out of bed until seven.) So Rachel, Alice, Karen, Peter and Hannah are miserable with anticipation.
Photographer:
Nick Kelsh

Hallelujah: Mom and Dad are up. Time to go downstairs and open presents. Barely able to contain her own excitement, Rachel helps Peter down the stairs.

The Rowley living room at 6:45 a.m., Christmas morning.

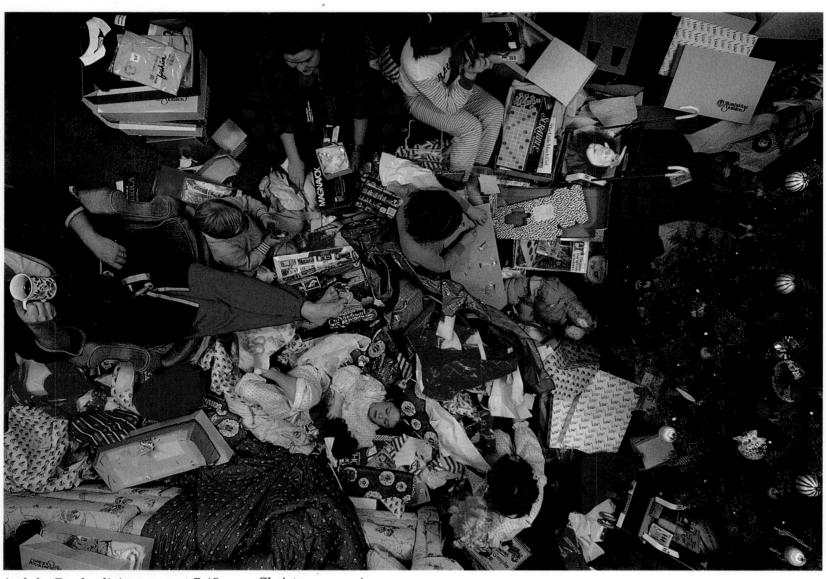

And the Rowley living room at 7:45 a.m., Christmas morning.

Ruff-housing: Golden Retriever Clancy and his playmate Patrick Dymond on Christmas Day in Pennsauken, New Jersey.
Photographer:
Gerald Seone Williams, *Philadelphia Inquirer*

When the children have been good,
That is, be it understood,
Good at meal-times, good at play,
Good all night, and good all day,
They shall have the pretty things
Merry Christmas always brings.
            —English proverb, 1850.

Seth Harvey, 6, of Manchester, Massachusetts, is rewarded with that great old standby, a Lionel train set.
Photographer:
David Alan Harvey, *National Geographic*

T hree-month-old Maxime Rene Michon Rollens
celebrates his first Christmas in Hollywood,
California.
Photographer:
Douglas Kirkland, *Sygma*

Patrick Dymond's grandmother thought the doll looked a lot like Patrick. And strangely enough, the doll was *named* Patrick by the manufacturer. So, on Christmas morning at grandmother's house in Pennsauken, New Jersey, "Patrick" meets Patrick while Mom and Dad wait for a reaction.
Photographer:
Gerald Seone Williams, *Philadelphia Inquirer*

A traditional Japanese feast awaits family guests at Sakura Residence in San Jose, California. The residence was organized to keep these elderly ladies, all of them born in Japan, together and out of commercial rest homes.

From left to right: Miyo Takata, Tei Iwanaga, Juto Yoshida, Eiko Kobayashi, Sumi Oka, Tsuma Yamanaka, and Kimi Kuwano.

Photographer:
Judy Griesedieck, *San Jose Mercury News*

Celtic fan Raymond Flynn is also the mayor of Boston and a very busy man at Christmastime. He spent Christmas Eve visiting homeless shelters in the city and Christmas morning hosting a breakfast attended by Irish, Haitian, Vietnamese and Cambodian immigrants. In the afternoon, he returns to his family's South Boston home.

Photographer:
Stan Grossfeld, *Boston Globe*

L auren and Ashley Cobb love their new Cabbage Patch dolls. Santa gave them the dolls for Christmas, and then their famous aunt, *National Geographic* photographer Jodi Cobb, took their picture.
Photographer:
Jodi Cobb, *National Geographic*

California dreamin': Five-year-old Emily sports her Christmas spoils in the living room of her Menlo Park, California, home. The photo is courtesy of her aunt Judy.
Photographer:
Judy Griesedieck, *San Jose Mercury News*

Curtis Battle has been taking care of Cynthia Forrest and her one-year-old son Brandon for several months, though it's getting harder and harder. Throughout the month of December, they've been living in his car. Here, they're having Christmas dinner "at home" in a parking lot in Venice Beach, California.

Formerly a fast-food restaurant manager in Washington, D.C., Battle has been looking for work in Los Angeles for four months. Earlier in the day, the family had lunch at the Union Rescue Mission in downtown Los Angeles, where volunteers gave Brandon some candy canes and a doll.
Photographer:
Rick Rickman, *Orange County Register*

enu: Turkey and cornbread dressing with giblet gravy, cranberry sauce, Southern greenbeans, Jack Daniel's Tipsy Sweet Potatoes ("People kill for second helpings"), macaroni and cheese, scalloped oyster casserole, homemade yeast rolls, country ham, fried okra, fresh coconut cake, boiled custard spiced with Jack Daniel's Tennessee Whisky. Location: Miss Mary Bobo's Boarding House, Lynchburg, Tennessee. Proprietress: Jack Daniel's nephew's grandniece, Miss Lynne Tolley.
Photographer:
Robin Hood

T here are no rich and no poor among us," says one Hutterite. "Life should be mostly joy," says another.

In the communal dining hall (*above*) at the 350-member Hutterian colony in Norfolk, Connecticut, Lillian Marchant gives Giles Clement a lift so he can light a candle on the Advent wreath. Like all women in the community, Lillian wears a long skirt and a dotted scarf. Later, in another room (*right*), the adults sit down to dinner.

The Connecticut Hutterite community is one of 300 in North America. This Christian, communally organized way of life was developed in Germany in the early 20th century. Though they spurn the commercialism and violence of American society, the Hutterites are not averse to such modern amenities as video cameras, microwave ovens and computers. The Hutterites try to balance communalism and individual free will. For instance, children do not become baptized members of the community until they reach college age and are ready to choose for themselves.

Photographer:
Brad Clift, *Hartford Courant*

At about 5:00 p.m. on Christmas Day, nurse Paula Graf quiets one-day-old Morganne Nicole Knoop at Norton Hospital in Louisville, Kentucky.

Nurse Graf sewed 50 tiny red outfits for all the babies born around Christmas. For the boys she fashioned red vests, bowties and caps; for the girls, caps and dresses.
Photographer:
Bill Luster
Louisville Courier-Journal

Christmas Quartet: Three-month-old David, Kathryn, Benjamin and Gregory Vanderwoude line up on the laps of their parents, Chris and Phil, for this Christmas Day portrait in Grand Rapids, Michigan.

As Christmas morning grows near, young people everywhere tremble with anticipation at the thought of what St. Nick might leave them under the tree. We thought that it would be only natural, then, to see how Christmas looks through a child's eyes. With the help of WNYC's *Kids America* and the National 4-H Council, Kodak sent film to kids of all ages all across the United States. The results of their efforts, a young person's view of the holiday season, is spread across these two pages.

Rebecca Heidt, 18   Atlanta, Ga.

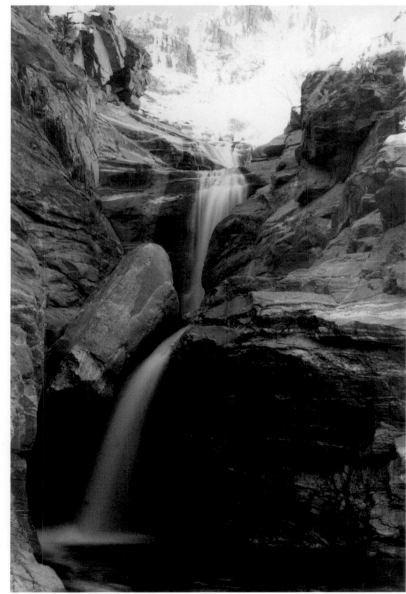

Jeff Ayer, 18   Tuscon, Ariz.

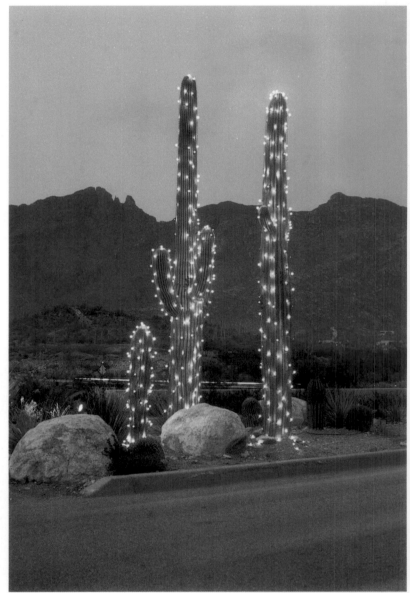

Jeff Ayer, 18   Tuscon, Ariz.

Gregory Foulds, 12   North Andover, Mass.

Heidi Palm, 17   **Grove City, Minn.**

Eduardo Toral, 13   **Madison, Wis.**   **Megan Redding, 13**   **Andover, Mass.**   **Jacob Barss-Bailey, 6**   **Lancaster, Mass.**

Jonathon Bauer, 11   **Rochester, N.Y.**   **Jeff Walters, 18**   **Lawrence, Kans.**

173

Heidi Palm, 17   **Grove City, Minn.**

Eduardo Toral, 13   **Madison, Wis.**   **Megan Redding, 13**   **Andover, Mass.**   **Jacob Barss-Bailey, 6**   **Lancaster, Mass.**

Jonathon Bauer, 11   **Rochester, N.Y.**   **Jeff Walters, 18**   **Lawrence, Kans.**

Early morning near Bigelow, Minnesota.

Lineage: The Dallas Cowboys' line crew is actually one big family. J. W. Smith (*center*) is uncle to the rest of the chain gang, which includes cousins (*left to right*) James Tyler, Bradley Bradshaw, Wilson Smith, Jon Beeler and Loren Bradshaw.

In honor of the season, the men add a yuletide touch to their uniforms for the Dallas-St. Louis contest. The Cowboys clipped the Cardinals, 21-16.
Photographer:
William Snyder, *Dallas Morning News*

The Zerby clan gathers in St. Paul, Minnesota, for dinner and TV football.
Photographer:
April Saul, *Philadelphia Inquirer*

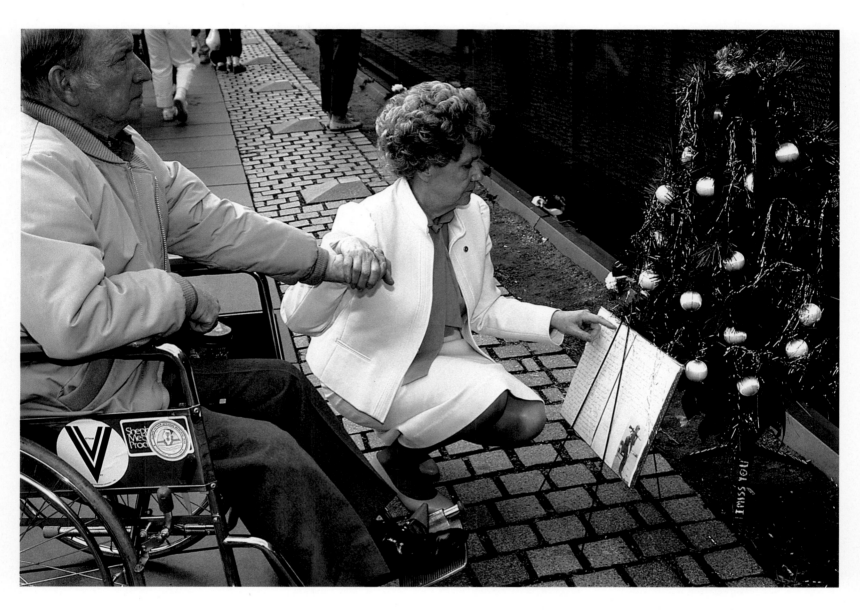

Every year, Russell and Eleanor Wimbish bring a Christmas tree to the Vietnam Veterans Memorial in Washington, D.C. The tree is for Eleanor's son, William Stocks, an Army sergeant who died in a helicopter crash in Vietnam on February 13, 1969.
Photographer:
Sal Lopes

At CNN Center in Atlanta, graphic artist Jim Powell works through Christmas Day preparing the "over-the-shoulder box" visible on the monitors. At broadcast time, the artwork will appear over the shoulder of the anchorperson who, in this case, will be reporting on Christmas festivities aboard U.S. Navy ships patrolling the Persian Gulf.
Photographer:
Scott Robinson
Atlanta Constitution and Journal

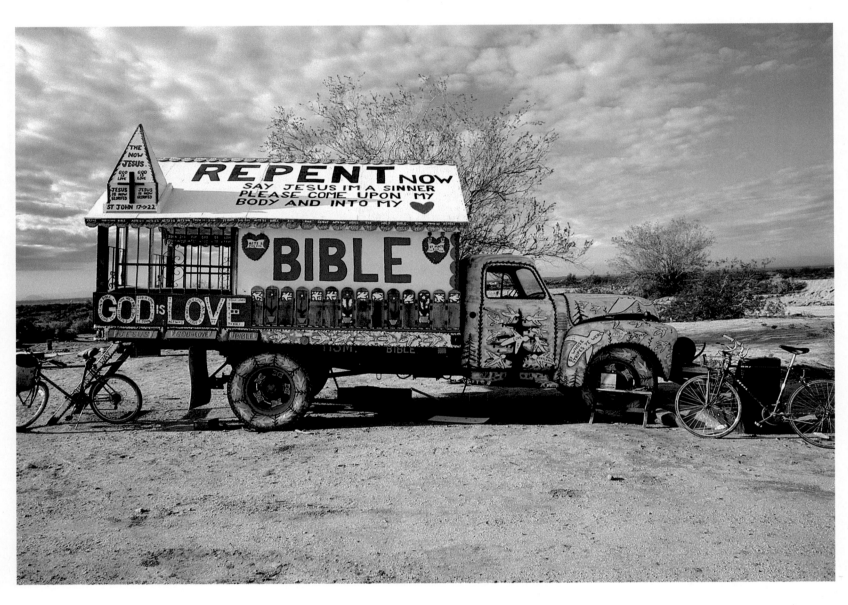

While on assignment for *Christmas in America*, photographer George Steinmetz ran across this unlikely Christian tableau in the California desert.
Photographer:
George Steinmetz

Larger than life: A Sony Jumbotron screen amplifies Dr. Robert H. Schuller for thousands of holiday season worshipers at the Crystal Cathedral in Garden Grove, California.

Schuller has built a huge stay-at-home congregation via his weekly, nationally televised church service, called the "Hour of Power." A mainline Protestant, Schuller preaches a theology of self-esteem and avoids fire-and-brimstone televangelism, as well as politics. The goal of ministry, the theologian/psychologist says, is to "find a hurt and heal it, find a need and fill it."
Photographer:
Joy Wolf, *Picture Group*

In 1776, Christmas feasting and drinking was considered by many colonists to be a decadent European tradition. On the night of December 25, British and Hessian troops stationed in Trenton, New Jersey, were so preoccupied with holiday revels, in fact, that they failed to post the necessary guards. It was an oversight that helped General Washington and his army rout the garrison the following morning after a surreptitious crossing from the Pennsylvania side of the Delaware River.

Washington's daring raid is reenacted every year on Christmas Day by the citizens of Bucks County, Pennsylvania.
Photographer:
Michael Mancuso
The Times (Trenton, N. J.)

A farmhouse along the White River in Meeker, Colorado. With temperatures hovering around -20° F, moisture from the river freezes into a smoky haze of ice particles.
Photographer:
James Balog

At the Skyline Convalescent Hospital in San Jose, California, Corinne Patterson, 85, spends the morning of December 16 filling in a crossword puzzle. Corinne has no immediate family, and her affairs are managed by a social worker.

Corinne looks forward to the decoration contests, the Christmas Eve party and the traditional Christmas dinner that will enliven the quiet hospital in the days ahead.
Photographer:
Judy Griesedieck, *San Jose Mercury News*

The dayes are very short, the year grows old,
Come, make a blazing fire, the weather is cold,
And fill up a full cup of nut brown beere,
Let's thaw our noses and our hearts upcheere,
For mery Christmas comes but once a year.
                    —*English proverb, 1693.*

A one-horse open sleigh glides across a meadow in central Vermont.
Photographer:
Ira Block, *Image Bank*

On the frozen Mississippi at Harriet Island, St. Paul, Minnesota.

Dusk in Madison, Wisconsin.

A Ghost of Christmas Past: This painted figure of Jesus was found in 1985 on a hill outside the mining town of Madrid, New Mexico. During the 1930s, the little town (pronounced *Mad*-rid) was famous for its opulent Christmas lights and giant illuminated biblical scenes. Transcontinental airline pilots flew low over the town, tipping the planes' wings so passengers could marvel at the sights below. The displays ended with World War II and were never revived.
Photographer:
Eduardo Fuss

San Jose, California's "Christmas in the Park" disappears onto the back of a truck. It will be stored for use again next year.
Photographer:
Judy Griesedieck, *San Jose Mercury News*

Juan Nardo spends part of Christmas Day sweeping the ballroom at
Miami Beach's famous Fontainebleau Hotel.

Firefighters in Los Alamitos, California, end the Christmas season with their own tree-lighting ceremony, a ritual that has become a community event in Orange County. This burning attracts hundreds of spectators and involves about 5,000 trees.
Photographer:
Rick Rickman
Orange County Register

New York's Old Westbury Gardens await the arrival of warmer days.
Photographer:
Elizabeth Billhardt

It's 2:30 a.m., December 25, and Old St. Nick is worn out. With good reason. He has to deliver gifts to children all around the world. And, despite the skepticism of a highly skeptical, highly commercial age, he must embody all the goodwill, generosity and optimism of America's Christmas season. It's a tough job, but yes, Virginia, there is a Santa Claus.
Photographer:
P. Kevin Morley
Richmond Times-Dispatch and News Leader

The Photographers

1 Eddie Adams
2 Daniel Aubry
3 Alexandra Avakian
  Woodfin Camp & Assoc.
4 Bill Ballenberg
5 Nina Barnett
6 Nicole Bengiveno
  New York Daily News
7 Susan Biddle
  Denver Post
8 Karen T. Borchers
  San Jose Mercury News
9 Torin Boyd
  Gamma
10 Jim Brandenburg
  National Geographic
11 Gary S. Chapman
  Louisville Courier-Journal
12 Paul Chesley
  Photographers/Aspen
13 Brad Clift
  Hartford Courant
14 Jack Corn
  Chicago Tribune
15 Lee Crum
16 William DeKay
  Detroit Free Press
17 Jay Dickman
  Denver Post
18 J. B. Diederich
  Contact Press Images
19 Don Doll, S.J.
  Creighton University
20 Misha Erwitt
  New York Daily News
21 Peter Essick
  University of Missouri
22 Melissa Farlow
  Pittsburgh Press
23 Dana Fineman
  Sygma
24 Victor Fisher
25 Kenneth Garrett
26 Jim Gensheimer
  San Jose Mercury News
27 Diego Goldberg
  Sygma
28 Judy Griesedieck
  San Jose Mercury News
29 Stan Grossfeld
  Boston Globe
30 Skeeter Hagler
  Dallas Times Herald
31 Peter Haley
  Tacoma Morning News Tribune
32 David Alan Harvey
  National Geographic

33 Robin Hood
34 John Isaac
  United Nations
35 Elaine Isaacson
  Orange County Register
36 Kenneth Jarecke
  Contact Press Images
37 Lynn Johnson
  Black Star
38 Frank Johnston
  Washington Post
39 Ed Kashi
40 Karen Kasmauski
  Wheeler Pictures
41 Larry Kasperek
  Birmingham Post Herald
42 Shelly Katz
  Time
43 Nick Kelsh
44 Norm Kerr
  Eastman Kodak
45 Douglas Kirkland
  Sygma
46 Paul Kitagaki, Jr.
  San Jose Mercury News
47 Kim Komenich
  San Francisco Examiner
48 Jean-Pierre Laffont
  Sygma
49 John Land Le Coq
50 Sarah Leen
  Philadelphia Inquirer
51 David Leeson
  Dallas Morning News
52 Andy Levin
53 Michelle Litvin
  Newsweek
54 Sal Lopes
55 Jimi Lott
  Seattle Times
56 Bill Luster
  Louisville Courier-Journal
57 James Magdanz
  Alaska Department of Fish and Game
58 Michael Melford
59 Doug Menuez
  Picture Group
60 Christopher Morris
  Black Star
61 Matthew Naythons
  Time
62 Seny Norasingh
63 Tony O'Brien
  Picture Group
64 Richard Olsenius
65 Randy Olson
  Pittsburgh Press
66 Graeme Outerbridge
67 Rick Peterson
68 Bill Pierce
  Time
69 Joanna B. Pinneo
  Foreign Mission Board

70 Larry C. Price
  Philadelphia Inquirer
71 Louis Psihoyos
  Contact Press Images
72 Alon Reininger
  Contact Press Images
73 Roger Ressmeyer
74 Mark Richards
  Picture Group
75 Jim Richardson
76 Rick Rickman
  Orange County Register
77 Steve Ringman
  San Francisco Chronicle
78 Scott Robinson
  Atlanta Constitution and Journal
79 Joe Rossi
  St. Paul Pioneer Press and Dispatch
80 Galen Rowell
81 April Saul
  Philadelphia Inquirer
82 Nicholas H. Sebastian
  Worldwide Images
83 Olga Shalygin
  Los Angeles Daily News
84 George Skene
  Orlando Sentinel
85 William Snyder
  Dallas Morning News
86 Paul Solomon
  Wheeler Pictures
87 Pamela K. Spaulding
  Louisville Courier-Journal
88 George Steinmetz
89 C. Scott Takushi
  St. Paul Pioneer Press and Dispatch
90 Medford Taylor
  Black Star
91 Patrick Tehan
  Orange County Register
92 David C. Turnley
  Detroit Free Press
93 Peter Turnley
  Newsweek
94 Jerry Valente
95 Jon Warren
96 Wendy Watriss
  Woodfin Camp & Assoc.
97 Bill Wax
98 Dan White
99 Karen Elshout Whiteley
  St. Louis Post-Dispatch
100 Gerald Seone Williams
  Philadelphia Inquirer
101 Zane B. Williams
102 Michael S. Wilson
103 Lance E. Wynn
  Grand Rapids Press

• Ely/10

• Milbridge/53

• Colebrook/66

• Freeport/53

• Spragueville/44

Yellowstone National Park/7

• Minneapolis/64

• St. Paul/79,81,89

• Marshall/79

• Rochester/79

• Bigelow/79

• St. Francis/19

• Rochester/44

• Boston/29

• Manchester • Cape Cod/24,29

• Hartford/13

• Norfolk/13

• Vassar/103

• Greenville/16

• Grand Rapids/103

• Madison/101

• Detroit/16,42

• Suffern/9
• Norwalk/6,13
• Greenwich/6,53
• Syracuse
• Yonkers/60
• Paramus/5
• Morristown/34
• Pennsauken
• New York/2,9,20,23,24,
  27,34,36,48,52,58,60,71,
  86,94
• Summit/71
• Long Island/73
• Hopewell/86
• Cassfield/5
• Philadelphia/43,50,70,100
• Bucks County
• Haddonfield/81
• Salem/43

• Fremont/92,93

• Aliquippa/22

• Chicago/89

• Bucyrus/103

• Pittsburgh/22,65,68

• Omaha/19,36

• Lincoln/36

• Beatrice/98

• Meeker

• Denver/17,75

• Aspen/12

• Colorado Springs/17

• Kansas City/98

• Columbia/21

• St. Louis/99

• Hermann/98

• New Albany/11

• Louisville/11,56,87

• Paoli/22

• Shakertown/56

• Santa Claus/56

• Harpers Ferry/102

• Richmond/69 • Wilmington

• Washington, D.C./4,25,38,
  40,54,82,102

• Fredericksburg/25

• Warsaw/25

• Kilmarnock/90

• Norfolk/40

• Virginia Beach/32

• Lynchburg/4

• Santa Fe/63

• Sumner County/14

• Kingsport/11

• Nashville/33 • Norris/33

• Winston-Salem/62

• Charlotte/72

• Lynchburg/33

• West Memphis/4

• Lubbock/70

• Wichita Falls/70

• Atlanta/78

• Birmingham/41

• Demopolis/41

• Montgomery/41

• Abilene/96

• Dallas/30,42,51,85

• Anderson/96

• Gramercy/15

• New Orleans/15

• Pasadena/93

• Orlando/1,84

• Tarpon Springs/62

• Winter Haven/84

• Sarasota/84

• Coral Springs/37

• Miami Beach/18,97

• Islamorada Key/18

Sponsors and Contributors

Thanks to:

Sponsors

Eastman Kodak Co.
K mart
Pan Am
Federal Express

Contributors

Adobe Systems, Inc.
Aldus Corporation
Apple Computer, Inc.
Barneyscan Corporation
Church of the Nativity
Dr. Robert H. Schuller & the Crystal Cathedral
  Congregation
Electronic Publishing Services
Express Package Systems, Inc.
Greater Houston Convention & Visitors Bureau
Grosvenor House Apartments
Kids America
Lighthouse Church of God & Christ
Lightspeed
L' Image Photo Lab, Inc.
Living Videotext Corporation
Lundeen & Associates
Metropolitan Life Insurance
Microprint
Mission Communities of Holy Family Parish
Moniterm Corporation
National 4-H Council
Our Lady of Guadalupe Church
Pallas Photo Lab, Inc.
Pan Am Building
Spofford Juvenile Center
St. Catherine's Church of Greenwich
SuperMac Technology
The Big Apple Circus
WNYC

Jeff Abbaticcio
Don Abood
Tom Adkinson
Jeff Allen
Bob Ambriano
Walter Anderson
Susan Andrews
Rich Andrews
Joseph Antonini
Al Apodaca
Ofelia Aquino
Ramon Araya
Bonnie Arnold
Allen Bachman
Monica Baltz
Anna Maria Bambara
Martha Bardach
Richard & Diana Barker
  & Family
Jeanne Bayer
Fr. Albert Bauman,
  O.S.B.
Dennis Beal
J. L. & Juanita Beasley
David Beckwith
David Benson Family
Jesse Birnbaum
Fr. Jose Maria Blanc
Britt Blaser
Herb Bleiweiss
Gene Blumberg
Ann Marie Boivie
Rachel Bolton
Liz Bond
Angela Bordon
Erik Boyd
Linda Boyes
Roger Brashears, Jr.
Clinton Breckridge
Kandes Bregman
Bart Brittain
Wallace Bronner
Deacon John Brooks
Thomas Brown
Marisa Bulzone
Diane Burns
Don Cable
Wendy Cacacie
Anthony Calcagno
Robert Cameron
Todd Cameron
Woodfin Camp
David Carriere
John Mack Carter
Mike Cerre
Maya Chernyak
Mary Chesterfield
Judy Ann Christensen
Albert Chu
Rachel Cobb

Gail Cohen
Hannnah & Norman
  Cohen
Christophe Colbert
Frank Collins
Sandy Colton
Debby Comiskey
Vicki Comiskey
Jim Connett
Sue Contois
Jennifer Cook
Ed Cooper
Patrick & Dorothy
  Corbett
Jim Cornacchia
Jennifer Corrigan
Merrill Creekmore
Beth Crowell
Larrie Curry
Steven Curtis
Jim Dau
Alan Davies
Jim Davis
Larry Davis
Bob DeCarlo
Kelly Decker
Mary Anne Decker
Cliff Deeds
Ray DeMoulin
Linda Dennery
Tom & Mary Jane Devine
Betty Dibartolomeo
Alan DiMarco
Chickie Dioguardi
Fred & Tuni Dixon
  & Family
Ron Dogey
Patrick Doherty
Miguel Dominguez, Ph.D.
Leon Donach
Craig Donahue
Debbie Donnelly
John Dougherty
Gene & Gayle Driskell
D.R. Ricky Duling
John Durniak
Van Mol Dye
Oscar Dystel
Mary Dawn Earley
Steve Edelman
Maura Eggan
Lynne Eich
Pat Ellerby
Connie Enzminger
Elliott Erwitt
Barbara Essick
Craig Evans
Bernard Fagan, S.J.
Bill Farley
Craig Farnum

Peter Feild
Vern Feild
Harlan Felt
Lisa Ferdinandsen
Mr. & Mrs. Ivan
  Filiatrault
Louise Finn
Frank Finnegan
Peter Fish
Peter Fishback
George Fisher
Flavio Flaviani
Dick Fleming
Charlotte Folkening
Paulette and Lazlo Fono
Ken Fossan
John Frank
Paulette Galle
Thomas A. Gara
Jesus J. Garcia
Simone Gaudin
Tom Geddie
Kent Gerken
Tara S. Gilani
Emmit Glanz
Louis Glazer
Michael Goldstein
Manuel Gombos
Linda Gomez
Sr. Angelina Gonzales
Emerson Goodwin
Jim Gordon
D. Gorton
George Greenfield
Millie Greig
Elaine Griffin
Tony Grigsbee
Bernard W. Groff
Joan Grossman
Don Guglielmino
Joe Guttierez
Annette Gutzmiedl
Catherine Gysin
Bernard Hagan
Dr. Clara Hale
Maj. C. C. Hall
Gregory Hall
Claus Halle
Cynthia Hallex
Steve Hansen
Sheila Hanson
Dean Hanson
Steve Haslett
Barbara Hawkins
Dina Hazan
Bonnie L. Heintz
Linda Hendrix
Manuel Hernandez
Andy Hertzfeld
John Hetterick

Dixie Hibbard
Preston Hibbard
Todd Hickson
James Higa
Kevin Hildebrand
Mike Holm
Twyla Holt
Ritchie Horowitz
Peter Howe
Cynthia Westbrook Hu
Peggie Ioppini
John Rice Irwin
Vern Iuppa
Charlie Jackson
Janice James
Joanne Jessie
Laura Jobin
Steve Jobs
Valtrey Johnson
Sr. Ramona Johnson
Charles Jones
Bill Joy
Larry Kanter
Jack Kardys
Susan Kare
Sheila Karnovsky
The Kell Family
The Reverends Kathy
 & Colin Kerr-Carpenter
Will Ketterson
Sharon Klaschka
Doreen & Fritz Klatt
Emily Klenk
Steve Knowlton
Jan Knox
Kent Kobersteen
Jeff Kriendler
Andrew Kruger
Bill Kuykendall
Tom Kyle
Mr. & Mrs. Philippe
 Lacoudre
Eliane Laffont
Ray Lake
Linda Lamb
Jerry Lawrence
Shari Lawrence
Mr. & Mrs. David
 Leading
John LeBosquet
John & Pam Leckie
Jim Leonard
Carleen Levasseur
Andy Levine
Chet Lewis
Ted Lewis
Ken Lieberman
Leslie Anne Liedtka
Nancy Littell
Jim Little & Family

Robin Lord
Barbara Loren
Mike Lotif
Patty Lucas
Glendon Lufkin
Tim Lundeen
Carolyn Mack
Judi Magann
Al Mandel
Marcy Mankoff
Joyce Mantyla
Thom Marchionna
Mike Marshall
Horace Marshall Family
Meg Martescello
Linda Mather
Joyce Matsumoto
Jed Mattes
Richard & Lucienne
 Matthews
James & Julie Matthias
Pat McCorkell, S.J.
Fallon McElliot
Carol McElroy
Pat McFerren
John & Judy McGarvey
Dan McGill
Warren McGlade
John McGlade
D. Pat McGuire
Mary McPherson
Naomi Medearis
Edwin Mellett
Lynda Mendez
Stan Menscher
Eric Meskauskis
Maria Miller
Melanie Miller
Richard Miller
Marla Milne
Pam Miracle
Deborah L. Mirams
Nancy Miscia
Ann Marie Molders
Art Mont
Richard Monta
Edmund Morales
Lynn Moratzka
Daize Biscaro Moreira
Stacy Morgan
Denise Morse
Ann Moscicki
Bruce Mowery
Robert Mullen
Deborah Munch
Lon Murphy
Nancy Nabors
Thomas Nigolian
Nick Nishida
Diane Norman

Kathy O'Connell
Dan O'Shea
Masaaki Okada
Clara & Elmer Olanna
Henri & Rita Olanna
Tony Oppenheim
Larry Orfaly
Celia Organista
Ava Osle
Paul Otomo
Paula Padilla
Richard Palazzo
Liz Palladino
Rusty Pallas
Rick Pappas
Seth Parelman
Larry Parkin
Dixie Marshall Parks
Dorraine Pate
Tyler Peppel
Liz Perle
Kenneth "Aku" Perreira
Naiken Perunal
Tatiana Petrovsky
The Reverend Peter
 Phavasiri, O.M.I.
David Pilgrim & Staff
Junette Pinkney
Jeanne & Larry Pinneo
Roger Pisani
Teobaldo H. Pla
Tom Plaskett
Robert Pledge
John Poimiroo
Elizabeth Pope
Carol Poston
Alison Pratt
Dan Procopio
Paul Pruneau
Jeff Pruss
Cherie Quaintance
Liz Quick
Eli Reed
Janet Reed
Alice M. Reid
Myra R. Reid
Dr. Lucy Reifel
Thomas P. Reilly
Ed Reingold
Andrew Rich
Lynda Richardson
Jan Roberts
Norman Roberts
Hugh & Rachel Rodgers
Robyn Roessler
Capt. John Rondon
Michael R. Rondou
Jack Rose
Terry Rosen
Jim Rowley

Lt. Noel Roy
Nancy Ruggeiro
Pat Ryan
Thomas Rykoff
Nola Safro
Sanjay Sakhuja
Janet Sakhuja
Marianne Samenko
Will & Marta Sanburn
Daniel Sare
David Sayre
Al Scamahorne
Tony Scaturro
Steve Scheier
Fred Scherrer
Cliff Schiappa
Bob Schneider
Kai Schuler
Marilyn Scofield
John Scully
Stuart Seaborn
Debbie Nye Sembler
Deborah Semel
Anne Seto
Kay Sexton
Neil & Karen Shakery
Laura Shultz
Mitch Silverberg
Joanne Sinnot
Doug Sleeter
Dorothea Smith
Peter Smith
Burrell Smith
Temple Smith
Tim Smith
Suzanne Soulié
Joe Spada
Mary Ellen Spanakos
Phil Sperr
David Spindler
Lynn Spivak
Jean Spivey
Lee Stalker
Dawn Stefan
Michelle Stephenson
Robert Stevens
Andy Stewart
Jim Stockton
Carlock Stooksbury
Blanche Streeter
Mary Strutz
Dick Stum
Danny Stupka
Ralph Subbiando
Peter Sutch
Rick Swig
Meg Switzgable
Jon Tandler
Christina A. Tasley
Michael Tchao

Mark Terry
Charles Thomas
Robert Tillman, S.J.
Jan Tipton
Diane Todd
Lynne & Margaret Tolley
Craig Tolman
Hipolito Torres
Anthony Totorici
Bill Tracy
Jean Tracy
The Troupers
Kim Tucker
Karen Tucker
Ruth Velozo
Liza Vicini
John Wade
Mr. & Mrs. James
 Waldron
Ruth Walsh
John Warnock
Greg Watkins
Dr. Jan Welle
Michael Wellman
Eric Weyenberg
Paul E. Wheeler
Ann White
Mr. & Mrs. Albert
 Whitehat
Diane Whitehurst
James Joseph Whiteley
Betty H. Willett
Michael Williams
 & Family
Ruth Williams Bennett
Joseph Wilson
Dave Winer
Philip Wong
Cathy Workman
Peter & Carolan
 Workman
Tom Wrubel
Chris Wurst
Amy Yamasaki
Mary Elizabeth Yost
Lisa Young
Bruce Young
Heidi Zimmerman

Staff

**Editor &
Project Director**
David Cohen

Associate Director
Rick Smolan

Managing Editor
Mark Rykoff

Associate Editor
Jennifer Erwitt

Art Director
Thomas K. Walker
GRAF/x

Writer
J. Curtis Sanburn

Assignment Editors
Torin Boyd
Devyani Kamdar
Ronald Pledge

Picture Editors
Bernard Boutrit
Woodfin Camp & Assoc.

Sandra Eisert
San Jose Mercury News

Frank Fournier
Contact Press Images

George Olson

Tom Porter
Orange County Register

George Wedding
Sacramento Bee

Production Director
Stephanie Sherman

Design Assistant
Dale Horstman

Copy Editors
Dorian Gossy
Amy Wheeler

Publicity Director
Patti Richards

Sponsorship Director
Cathy Quealy

Sales Director
Carole Bidnick

Finance Director
Stanford Hays

Sales Assistant
Kate Kelly

Office Manager
Lew Stowbunenko

Researchers
Laura Bleiberg
Clio McNicholl
Gloria Smolan

Lawyers
E. Gabriel Perle
New York

William Coblentz
San Francisco

**William Collins Sons &
Co., Ltd.**
F. Ian Chapman
Chairman

George Craig
Vice Chairman

Sonia Land
Group Finance Director

**Dai Nippon Printing
Co., Ltd.**
Ryo Chigira
Toshihiko Miyazaki
Yukio Yoshida
Takashi Ishikawa
Kosuke Tago
Kikuo Mori
Yuichiro Sato
Yoshiyasu Kosugi
Kimio Honda

Christmas in America was entirely designed and pro-
duced on an Apple Macintosh II computer equipped with
a Supermac Trinitron Monitor and Dataframe XP-60
hard disks. The images were input with a Barneyscan
and output on a Linotronic 300 printer. Project software
included Aldus Pagemaker, Living Videotext MORE, and
Microsoft Works. We gratefully acknowledge the assistance of Microprint and the companies listed on the pre-
vious pages for their generous contribution to this book.